ROLLER COASTER
LOG BOOK

This LogBook belongs to:

Copyright © 2021 CousinNta Press

All Rights Reserved, no part of this book may be used or reproduced by any means, graphic, electronic, or mechanical, including photocopying, recording, taping, or by any information storage retrieval system without the written permission of the publisher

Coaster Name

Visiting Date	Park Name	Location

Coaster / Track Type	My Ride Position	Lenght
	Front Back Middle	Height
		Top Speed

Number of Loops	Designer of Coaster	Year Opened

Wheather

Coaster Notes
How was your Coaster experience? What did you like about this coaster? Write down how you felt riding it, an any additional notes about this ride

Will Return once again?	Overall Experience
Yep / Nope	

Coaster Name

Visiting Date	**Park Name**	**Location**

Coaster / Track Type	**My RIde Position** Front Back Middle	Lenght Height Top Speed

Number of Loops	**Designer of Coaster**	**Year Opened**

Wheather

Coaster Notes

How was your Coaster experience? What did you like about this coaster? Write down how you felt riding it, an any additional notes about this ride

Will Return once again?	**Overall Experience**
Yep / Nope	☆☆☆☆☆

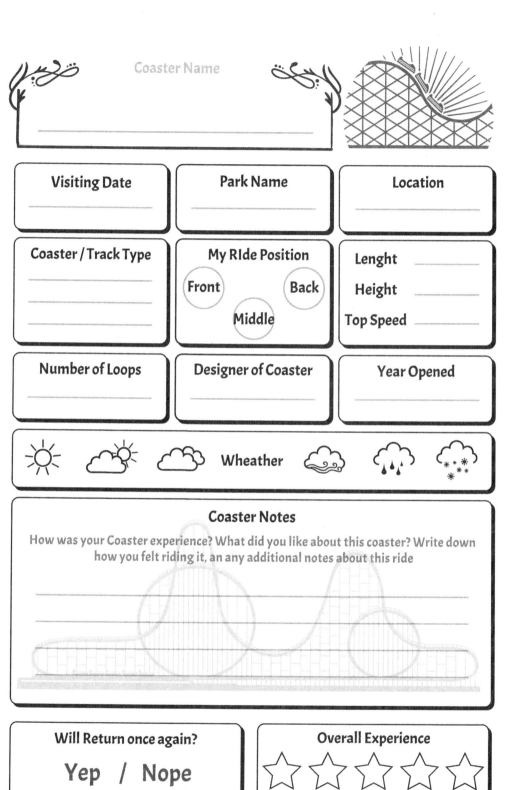

Coaster Name

Visiting Date	Park Name	Location

Coaster / Track Type	My Ride Position Front Back Middle	Lenght Height Top Speed

Number of Loops	Designer of Coaster	Year Opened

Wheather

Coaster Notes
How was your Coaster experience? What did you like about this coaster? Write down how you felt riding it, an any additional notes about this ride

---

Will Return once again?

Yep / Nope

Overall Experience

Coaster Name

Visiting Date

Park Name

Location

Coaster / Track Type

My RIde Position
Front   Back
Middle

Lenght
Height
Top Speed

Number of Loops

Designer of Coaster

Year Opened

Wheather

Coaster Notes

How was your Coaster experience? What did you like about this coaster? Write down
how you felt riding it, an any additional notes about this ride

Will Return once again?

Yep / Nope

Overall Experience

Coaster Name

Visiting Date

Park Name

Location

Coaster / Track Type

My RIde Position

Front   Back

Middle

Lenght

Height

Top Speed

Number of Loops

Designer of Coaster

Year Opened

Wheather

Coaster Notes

How was your Coaster experience? What did you like about this coaster? Write down how you felt riding it, an any additional notes about this ride

Will Return once again?

Yep / Nope

Overall Experience

☆ ☆ ☆ ☆ ☆

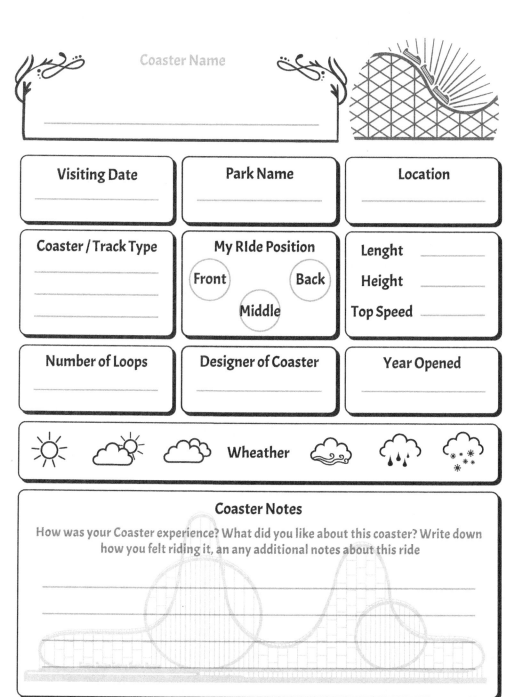

Coaster Name

| Visiting Date | Park Name | Location |

| Coaster / Track Type | My Ride Position — Front / Back / Middle | Lenght / Height / Top Speed |

| Number of Loops | Designer of Coaster | Year Opened |

Wheather

Coaster Notes
How was your Coaster experience? What did you like about this coaster? Write down how you felt riding it, an any additional notes about this ride

| Will Return once again? | Overall Experience |
| Yep / Nope |  |

Coaster Name

Visiting Date	Park Name	Location

Coaster / Track Type	My RIde Position	Lenght
	Front Back Middle	Height
		Top Speed

Number of Loops	Designer of Coaster	Year Opened

Wheather

Coaster Notes

How was your Coaster experience? What did you like about this coaster? Write down how you felt riding it, an any additional notes about this ride

Will Return once again?

Yep / Nope

Overall Experience

☆☆☆☆☆

Coaster Name

Visiting Date	Park Name	Location

Coaster / Track Type	My RIde Position	Lenght
	Front Back	Height
	Middle	Top Speed

Number of Loops	Designer of Coaster	Year Opened

Wheather

Coaster Notes

How was your Coaster experience? What did you like about this coaster? Write down how you felt riding it, an any additional notes about this ride

Will Return once again?

Yep / Nope

Overall Experience

Coaster Name

Visiting Date	**Park Name**	**Location**

Coaster / Track Type

My RIde Position

Front   Back

Middle

Lenght ___
Height ___
Top Speed ___

Number of Loops	**Designer of Coaster**	**Year Opened**

Wheather

Coaster Notes

How was your Coaster experience? What did you like about this coaster? Write down how you felt riding it, an any additional notes about this ride

Will Return once again?

Yep / Nope

Overall Experience

☆ ☆ ☆ ☆ ☆

Coaster Name

Visiting Date

Park Name

Location

Coaster / Track Type

My Ride Position
- Front
- Back
- Middle

Lenght
Height
Top Speed

Number of Loops

Designer of Coaster

Year Opened

Wheather

Coaster Notes
How was your Coaster experience? What did you like about this coaster? Write down how you felt riding it, an any additional notes about this ride

Will Return once again?
Yep / Nope

Overall Experience

Coaster Name

Visiting Date	Park Name	Location

Coaster / Track Type

My RIde Position
- Front
- Back
- Middle

Lenght
Height
Top Speed

Number of Loops	Designer of Coaster	Year Opened

Wheather

Coaster Notes

How was your Coaster experience? What did you like about this coaster? Write down how you felt riding it, an any additional notes about this ride

Will Return once again?

Yep / Nope

Overall Experience

☆ ☆ ☆ ☆ ☆

Coaster Name
_____

Visiting Date
_____

Park Name
_____

Location
_____

Coaster / Track Type
_____
_____
_____

My Ride Position
(Front)   (Back)
(Middle)

Lenght _____
Height _____
Top Speed _____

Number of Loops
_____

Designer of Coaster
_____

Year Opened
_____

☀️ ⛅ ☁️ **Wheather** 🌬️ 🌧️ ❄️

Coaster Notes

How was your Coaster experience? What did you like about this coaster? Write down how you felt riding it, an any additional notes about this ride

_____
_____
_____

Will Return once again?

Yep / Nope

Overall Experience

☆ ☆ ☆ ☆ ☆

Coaster Name

_____

Visiting Date	Park Name	Location

Coaster / Track Type

My RIde Position
(Front) (Back)
(Middle)

Lenght _____
Height _____
Top Speed _____

Number of Loops	Designer of Coaster	Year Opened

Wheather

Coaster Notes

How was your Coaster experience? What did you like about this coaster? Write down
how you felt riding it, an any additional notes about this ride

_____
_____
_____

Will Return once again?

Yep / Nope

Overall Experience
☆☆☆☆☆

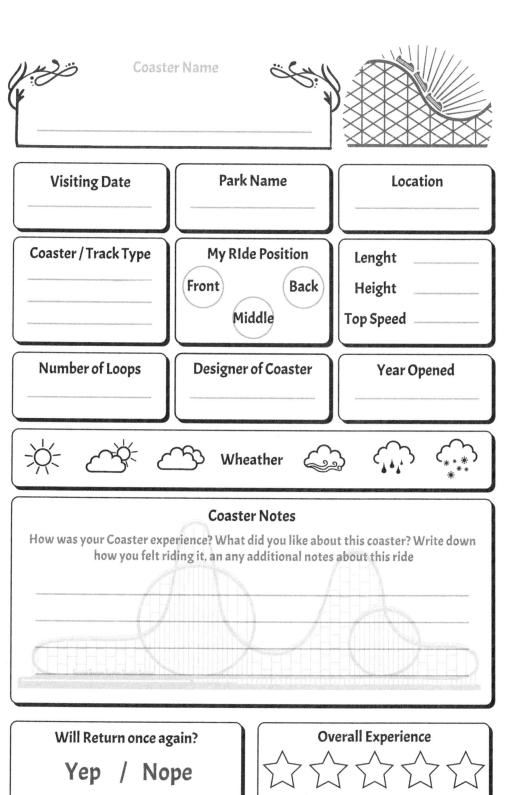

Coaster Name

_____

Visiting Date	**Park Name**	**Location**

Coaster / Track Type

My RIde Position

(Front)   (Back)
(Middle)

Lenght _____
Height _____
Top Speed _____

Number of Loops	**Designer of Coaster**	**Year Opened**

Wheather

Coaster Notes

How was your Coaster experience? What did you like about this coaster? Write down how you felt riding it, an any additional notes about this ride

_____
_____
_____

Will Return once again?

Yep / Nope

Overall Experience

☆ ☆ ☆ ☆ ☆

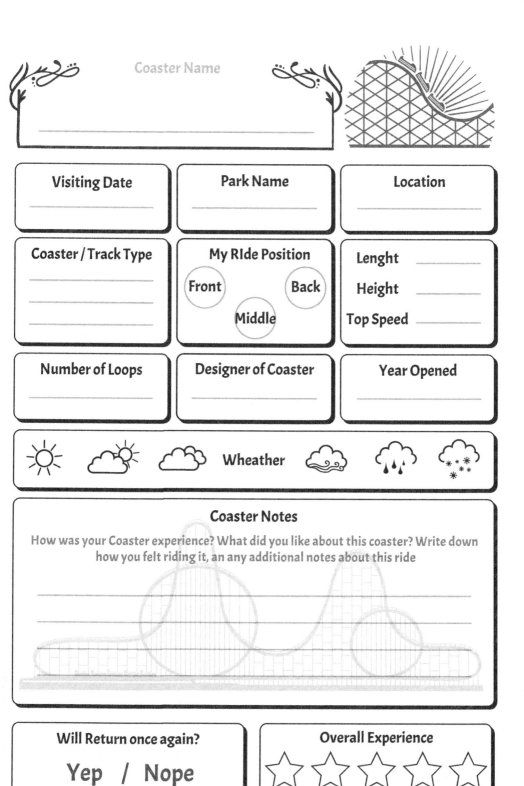

Coaster Name

Visiting Date

Park Name

Location

Coaster / Track Type

My RIde Position

Front   Back

Middle

Lenght

Height

Top Speed

Number of Loops

Designer of Coaster

Year Opened

Wheather

Coaster Notes

How was your Coaster experience? What did you like about this coaster? Write down how you felt riding it, an any additional notes about this ride

Will Return once again?

Yep / Nope

Overall Experience

☆ ☆ ☆ ☆ ☆

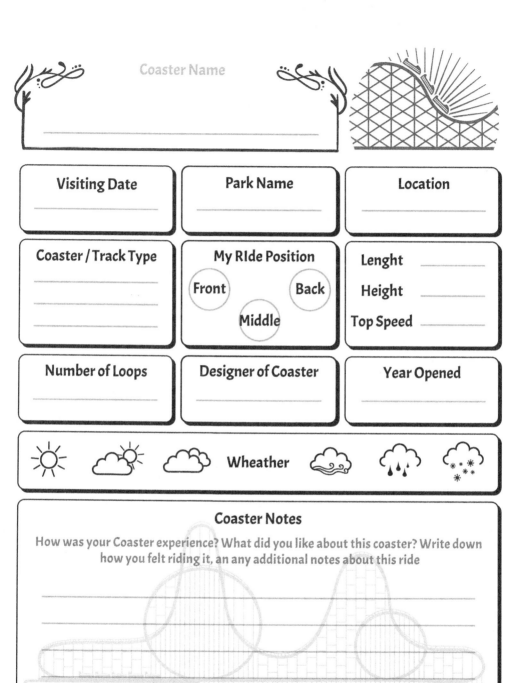

Coaster Name

| Visiting Date | Park Name | Location |

| Coaster / Track Type | My Ride Position — Front / Back / Middle | Lenght / Height / Top Speed |

| Number of Loops | Designer of Coaster | Year Opened |

Wheather

Coaster Notes
How was your Coaster experience? What did you like about this coaster? Write down how you felt riding it, an any additional notes about this ride

Will Return once again?
Yep / Nope

Overall Experience

Coaster Name

Visiting Date

Park Name

Location

Coaster / Track Type

My Ride Position
- Front
- Back
- Middle

Lenght
Height
Top Speed

Number of Loops

Designer of Coaster

Year Opened

Wheather

Coaster Notes
How was your Coaster experience? What did you like about this coaster? Write down how you felt riding it, an any additional notes about this ride

Will Return once again?
Yep / Nope

Overall Experience
☆ ☆ ☆ ☆ ☆

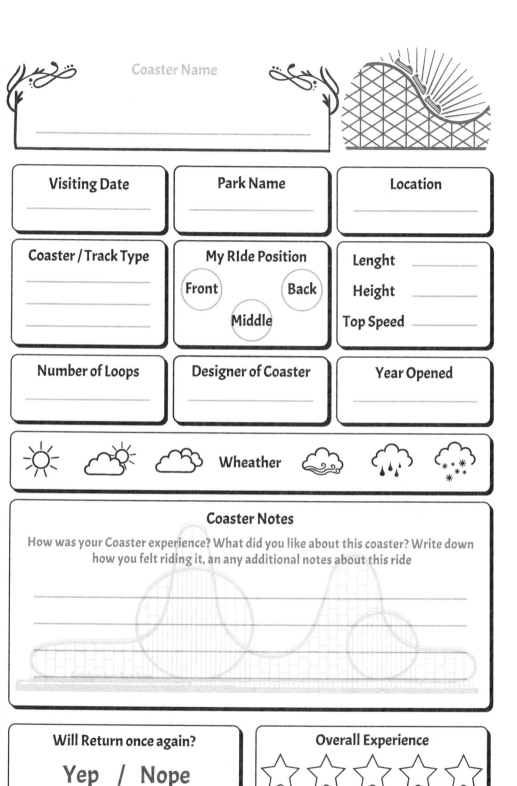

Coaster Name
_____

| Visiting Date | Park Name | Location |

Coaster / Track Type	My Ride Position	Lenght
	Front Back	Height
	Middle	Top Speed

| Number of Loops | Designer of Coaster | Year Opened |

Wheather

Coaster Notes

How was your Coaster experience? What did you like about this coaster? Write down how you felt riding it, an any additional notes about this ride

_____
_____
_____

Will Return once again?

Yep / Nope

Overall Experience

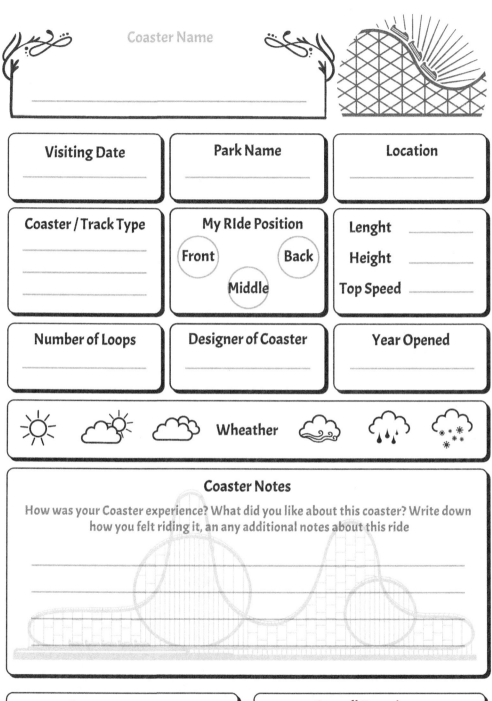

Coaster Name

Visiting Date

Park Name

Location

Coaster / Track Type

My RIde Position
(Front) (Back)
(Middle)

Lenght
Height
Top Speed

Number of Loops

Designer of Coaster

Year Opened

Wheather

Coaster Notes

How was your Coaster experience? What did you like about this coaster? Write down how you felt riding it, an any additional notes about this ride

Will Return once again?

Yep / Nope

Overall Experience

☆ ☆ ☆ ☆ ☆

Coaster Name

Visiting Date	Park Name	Location

Coaster / Track Type	My RIde Position Front Back Middle	Lenght Height Top Speed

Number of Loops	Designer of Coaster	Year Opened

Wheather

Coaster Notes

How was your Coaster experience? What did you like about this coaster? Write down how you felt riding it, an any additional notes about this ride

Will Return once again? Yep / Nope	Overall Experience 

Coaster Name

Visiting Date	Park Name	Location

Coaster / Track Type

My RIde Position
(Front) (Back) (Middle)

Lenght ___
Height ___
Top Speed ___

Number of Loops	Designer of Coaster	Year Opened

Wheather

Coaster Notes

How was your Coaster experience? What did you like about this coaster? Write down how you felt riding it, an any additional notes about this ride

Will Return once again?

Yep / Nope

Overall Experience

☆ ☆ ☆ ☆ ☆

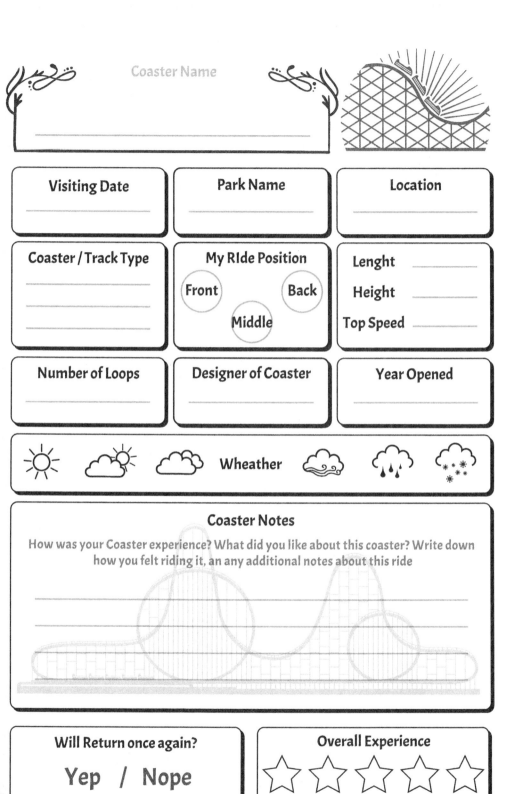

Coaster Name

Visiting Date

Park Name

Location

Coaster / Track Type

My Ride Position
- Front
- Back
- Middle

Lenght
Height
Top Speed

Number of Loops

Designer of Coaster

Year Opened

Wheather

Coaster Notes

How was your Coaster experience? What did you like about this coaster? Write down how you felt riding it, an any additional notes about this ride

Will Return once again?

Yep / Nope

Overall Experience

Coaster Name

Visiting Date	Park Name	Location

Coaster / Track Type	My RIde Position	Lenght
	Front Back Middle	Height
		Top Speed

Number of Loops	Designer of Coaster	Year Opened

Wheather

Coaster Notes

How was your Coaster experience? What did you like about this coaster? Write down how you felt riding it, an any additional notes about this ride

Will Return once again?	Overall Experience
Yep / Nope	☆ ☆ ☆ ☆ ☆

Coaster Name

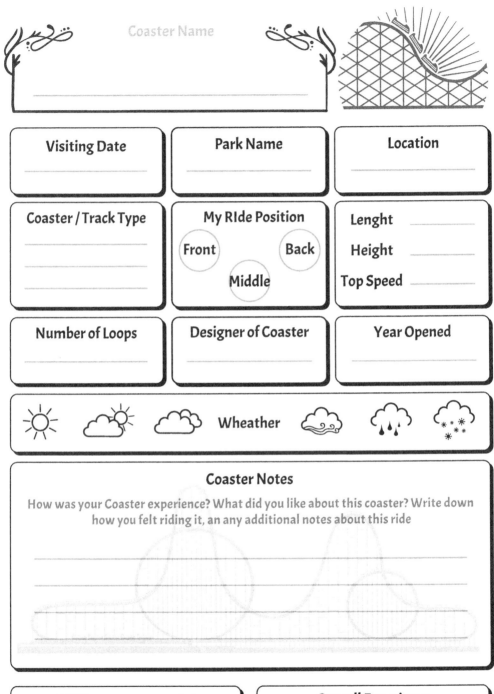

Visiting Date	Park Name	Location

Coaster / Track Type	My Ride Position Front Back Middle	Lenght Height Top Speed

Number of Loops	Designer of Coaster	Year Opened

Wheather

Coaster Notes

How was your Coaster experience? What did you like about this coaster? Write down how you felt riding it, an any additional notes about this ride

Will Return once again? Yep / Nope	Overall Experience 

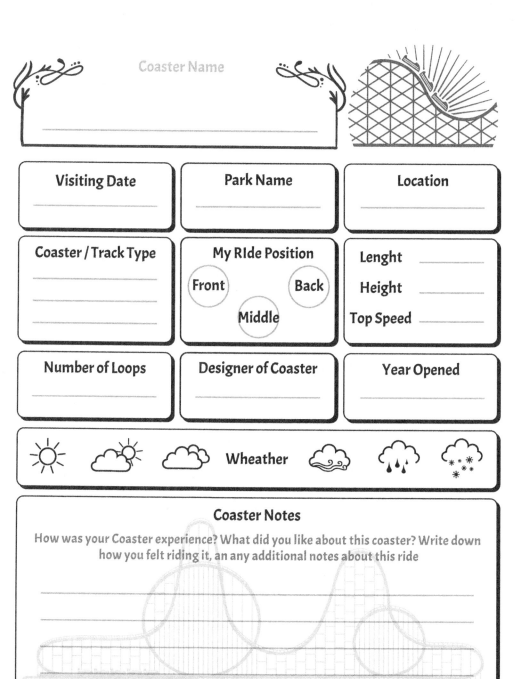

Coaster Name

Visiting Date

Park Name

Location

Coaster / Track Type

My RIde Position

Front

Back

Middle

Lenght

Height

Top Speed

Number of Loops

Designer of Coaster

Year Opened

Wheather

Coaster Notes

How was your Coaster experience? What did you like about this coaster? Write down how you felt riding it, an any additional notes about this ride

Will Return once again?

Yep / Nope

Overall Experience

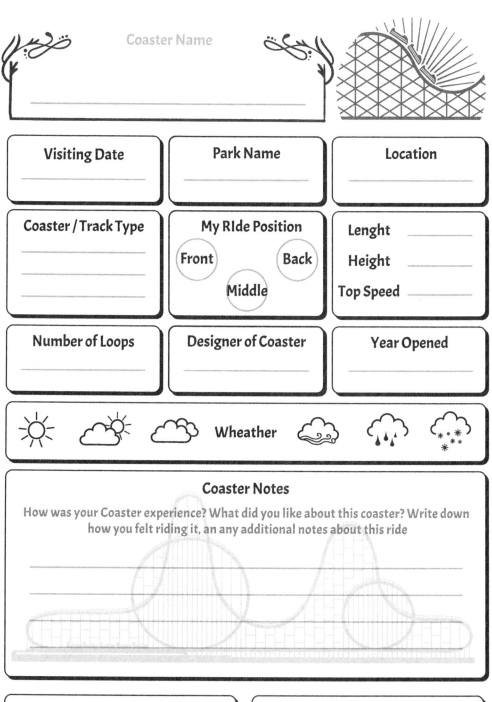

Coaster Name

Visiting Date

Park Name

Location

Coaster / Track Type

My Ride Position
- Front
- Back
- Middle

Lenght

Height

Top Speed

Number of Loops

Designer of Coaster

Year Opened

Wheather

Coaster Notes

How was your Coaster experience? What did you like about this coaster? Write down how you felt riding it, an any additional notes about this ride

Will Return once again?

Yep / Nope

Overall Experience

Coaster Name
_____

| Visiting Date | Park Name | Location |

Coaster / Track Type	My Ride Position	Lenght
	Front Back	Height
	Middle	Top Speed

| Number of Loops | Designer of Coaster | Year Opened |

☀️ ⛅ ☁️ Wheather 💨 🌧️ 🌨️

Coaster Notes

How was your Coaster experience? What did you like about this coaster? Write down how you felt riding it, an any additional notes about this ride

_____
_____
_____

Will Return once again?

Yep / Nope

Overall Experience

Coaster Name
_____

Visiting Date
_____

Park Name
_____

Location
_____

Coaster / Track Type
_____
_____
_____

My Ride Position
(Front)   (Back)
(Middle)

Lenght _____
Height _____
Top Speed _____

Number of Loops
_____

Designer of Coaster
_____

Year Opened
_____

☀ ⛅ ☁ **Wheather** 🌬 🌧 ❄

Coaster Notes

How was your Coaster experience? What did you like about this coaster? Write down how you felt riding it, an any additional notes about this ride

_____
_____
_____
_____

Will Return once again?

Yep / Nope

Overall Experience

☆ ☆ ☆ ☆ ☆

Coaster Name

Visiting Date

Park Name

Location

Coaster / Track Type

My RIde Position
Front Back Middle

Lenght
Height
Top Speed

Number of Loops

Designer of Coaster

Year Opened

Wheather

Coaster Notes

How was your Coaster experience? What did you like about this coaster? Write down how you felt riding it, an any additional notes about this ride

Will Return once again?

Yep / Nope

Overall Experience
☆ ☆ ☆ ☆ ☆

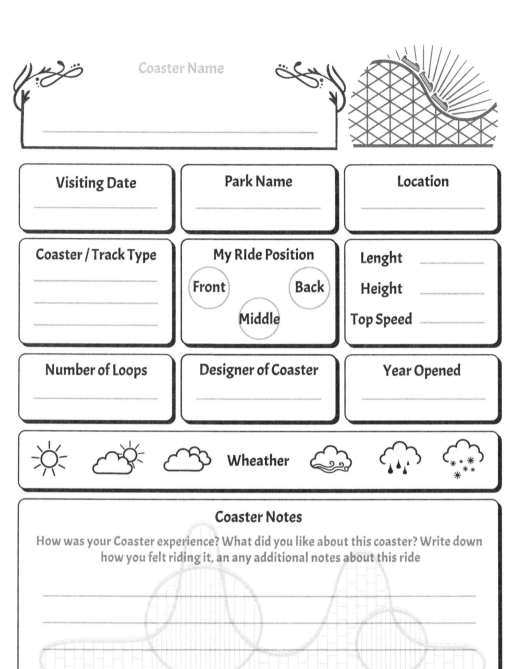

Coaster Name

Visiting Date	Park Name	Location

Coaster / Track Type	My Ride Position	Lenght
	Front Back Middle	Height
		Top Speed

Number of Loops	Designer of Coaster	Year Opened

Wheather

Coaster Notes

How was your Coaster experience? What did you like about this coaster? Write down how you felt riding it, an any additional notes about this ride

---

Will Return once again? Yep / Nope

Overall Experience

Coaster Name

Visiting Date

Park Name

Location

Coaster / Track Type

My RIde Position
Front
Back
Middle

Lenght

Height

Top Speed

Number of Loops

Designer of Coaster

Year Opened

Wheather

Coaster Notes

How was your Coaster experience? What did you like about this coaster? Write down how you felt riding it, an any additional notes about this ride

Will Return once again?

Yep / Nope

Overall Experience

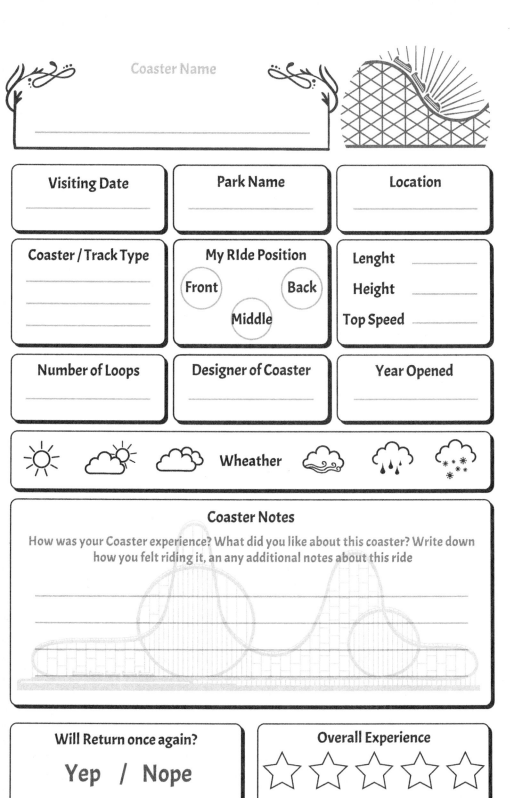

Coaster Name

Visiting Date

Park Name

Location

Coaster / Track Type

My RIde Position
Front   Back
Middle

Lenght
Height
Top Speed

Number of Loops

Designer of Coaster

Year Opened

Wheather

Coaster Notes

How was your Coaster experience? What did you like about this coaster? Write down how you felt riding it, an any additional notes about this ride

Will Return once again?
Yep / Nope

Overall Experience

Coaster Name

Visiting Date	Park Name	Location

Coaster / Track Type

My RIde Position
Front   Back
Middle

Lenght
Height
Top Speed

Number of Loops	Designer of Coaster	Year Opened

Wheather

Coaster Notes

How was your Coaster experience? What did you like about this coaster? Write down how you felt riding it, an any additional notes about this ride

Will Return once again?

Yep / Nope

Overall Experience
☆ ☆ ☆ ☆ ☆

Coaster Name

_____

Visiting Date	Park Name	Location

Coaster / Track Type

My RIde Position
(Front) (Back)
(Middle)

Lenght _____
Height _____
Top Speed _____

Number of Loops	Designer of Coaster	Year Opened

Wheather

Coaster Notes

How was your Coaster experience? What did you like about this coaster? Write down how you felt riding it, an any additional notes about this ride

_____
_____
_____

Will Return once again?

Yep / Nope

Overall Experience

☆ ☆ ☆ ☆ ☆

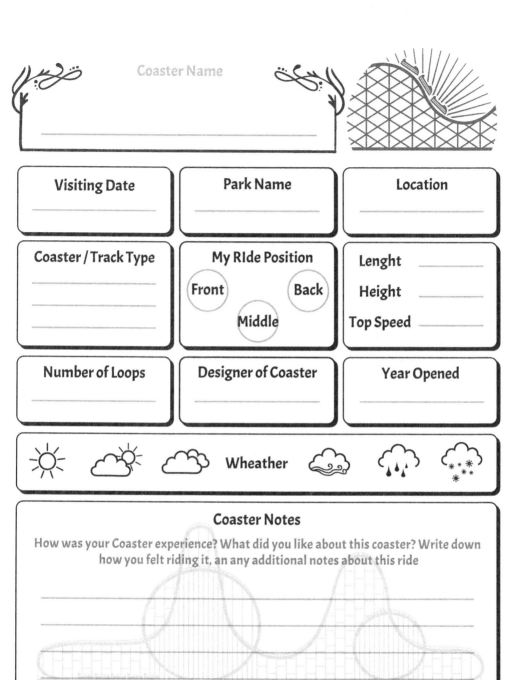

Coaster Name

Visiting Date

Park Name

Location

Coaster / Track Type

My RIde Position
Front   Back
Middle

Lenght
Height
Top Speed

Number of Loops

Designer of Coaster

Year Opened

Wheather

Coaster Notes

How was your Coaster experience? What did you like about this coaster? Write down how you felt riding it, an any additional notes about this ride

Will Return once again?

Yep / Nope

Overall Experience

Coaster Name

_____

Visiting Date	Park Name	Location

Coaster / Track Type

My Ride Position
- Front
- Middle
- Back

Lenght
Height
Top Speed

Number of Loops

Designer of Coaster

Year Opened

Wheather

Coaster Notes

How was your Coaster experience? What did you like about this coaster? Write down how you felt riding it, an any additional notes about this ride

_____
_____
_____

Will Return once again?

Yep / Nope

Overall Experience

Coaster Name

| Visiting Date | Park Name | Location |

Coaster / Track Type

My RIde Position
(Front) (Back) (Middle)

Lenght
Height
Top Speed

| Number of Loops | Designer of Coaster | Year Opened |

Wheather

Coaster Notes

How was your Coaster experience? What did you like about this coaster? Write down
how you felt riding it, an any additional notes about this ride

Will Return once again?

Yep / Nope

Overall Experience

Coaster Name

Visiting Date	Park Name	Location

Coaster / Track Type	My Ride Position	Length
	Front Back	Height
	Middle	Top Speed

Number of Loops	Designer of Coaster	Year Opened

☀️ ⛅ ☁️ **Wheather** 🌬️ 🌧️ 🌨️

Coaster Notes

How was your Coaster experience? What did you like about this coaster? Write down how you felt riding it, an any additional notes about this ride

---

Will Return once again?

Yep / Nope

Overall Experience

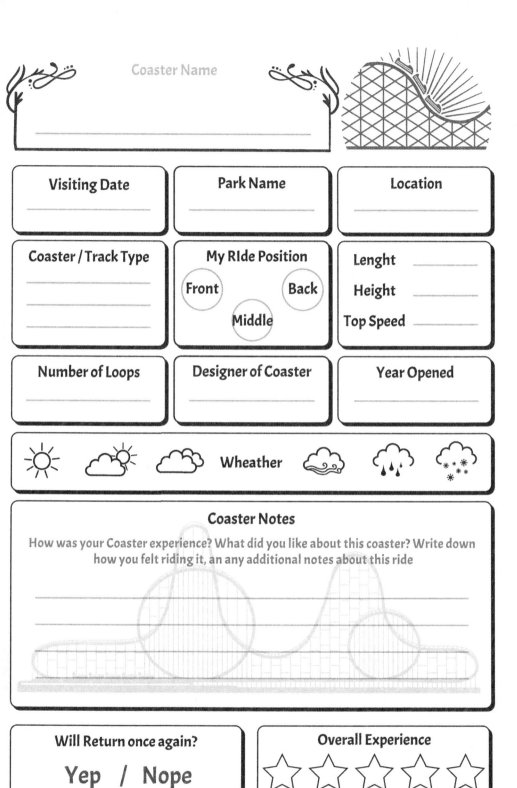

Coaster Name

Visiting Date

Park Name

Location

Coaster / Track Type

My RIde Position

Front   Back

Middle

Lenght

Height

Top Speed

Number of Loops

Designer of Coaster

Year Opened

Wheather

Coaster Notes

How was your Coaster experience? What did you like about this coaster? Write down how you felt riding it, an any additional notes about this ride

Will Return once again?

Yep / Nope

Overall Experience

☆ ☆ ☆ ☆ ☆

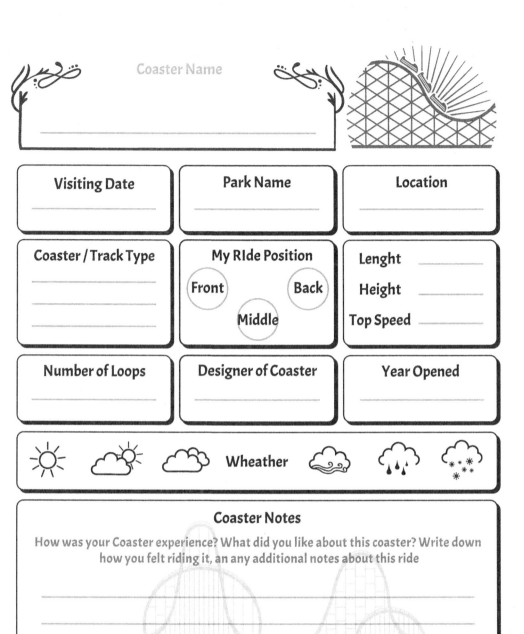

Coaster Name

Visiting Date	Park Name	Location

Coaster / Track Type

My RIde Position
(Front) (Back)
(Middle)

Lenght
Height
Top Speed

Number of Loops	Designer of Coaster	Year Opened

Wheather

Coaster Notes

How was your Coaster experience? What did you like about this coaster? Write down how you felt riding it, an any additional notes about this ride

Will Return once again?

Yep / Nope

Overall Experience

☆ ☆ ☆ ☆ ☆

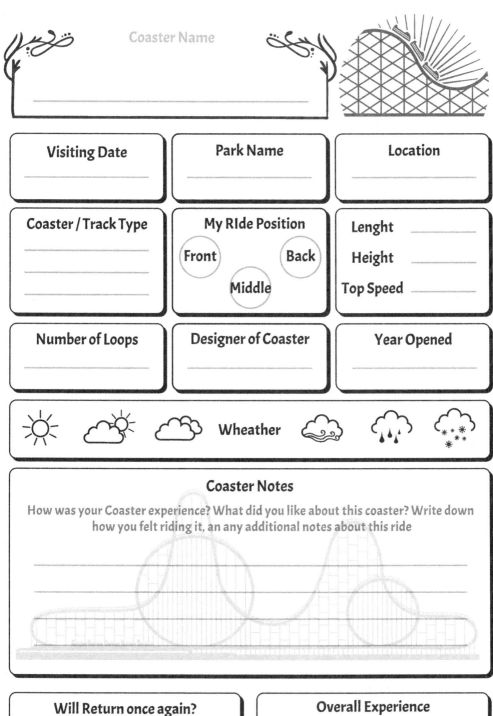

Coaster Name

_____

Visiting Date	Park Name	Location

Coaster / Track Type	My Ride Position	Lenght
	Front Back Middle	Height
		Top Speed

Number of Loops	Designer of Coaster	Year Opened

Wheather

Coaster Notes

How was your Coaster experience? What did you like about this coaster? Write down how you felt riding it, an any additional notes about this ride

_____
_____
_____

Will Return once again?

Yep / Nope

Overall Experience

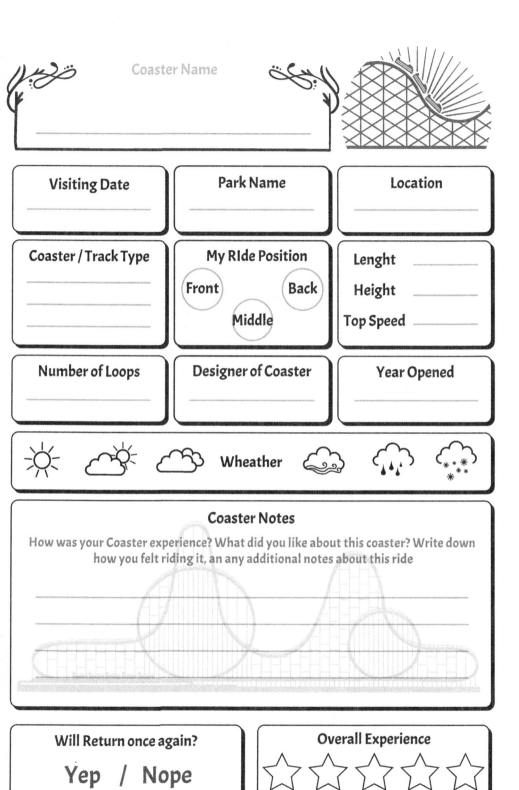

Coaster Name
_____

Visiting Date	Park Name	Location

Coaster / Track Type	My Ride Position	Lenght _____
	(Front) (Back)	Height _____
	(Middle)	Top Speed _____

Number of Loops	Designer of Coaster	Year Opened

☀️ ⛅ ☁️ Wheather 🌬️ 🌧️ 🌨️

Coaster Notes

How was your Coaster experience? What did you like about this coaster? Write down how you felt riding it, an any additional notes about this ride

_____
_____
_____

Will Return once again?

Yep / Nope

Overall Experience

☆ ☆ ☆ ☆ ☆

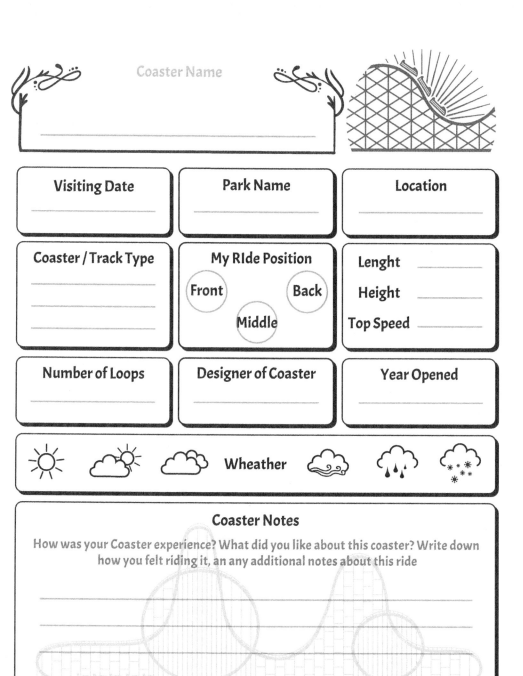

Coaster Name

| Visiting Date | Park Name | Location |

| Coaster / Track Type | My Ride Position — Front / Back / Middle | Lenght / Height / Top Speed |

| Number of Loops | Designer of Coaster | Year Opened |

Wheather

Coaster Notes
How was your Coaster experience? What did you like about this coaster? Write down how you felt riding it, an any additional notes about this ride

Will Return once again? Yep / Nope

Overall Experience ☆☆☆☆☆

Coaster Name
_____

Visiting Date
_____

Park Name
_____

Location
_____

Coaster / Track Type
_____
_____

My RIde Position
(Front)   (Back)
(Middle)

Lenght _____
Height _____
Top Speed _____

Number of Loops
_____

Designer of Coaster
_____

Year Opened
_____

Wheather

Coaster Notes

How was your Coaster experience? What did you like about this coaster? Write down how you felt riding it, an any additional notes about this ride

_____
_____
_____

Will Return once again?

Yep / Nope

Overall Experience

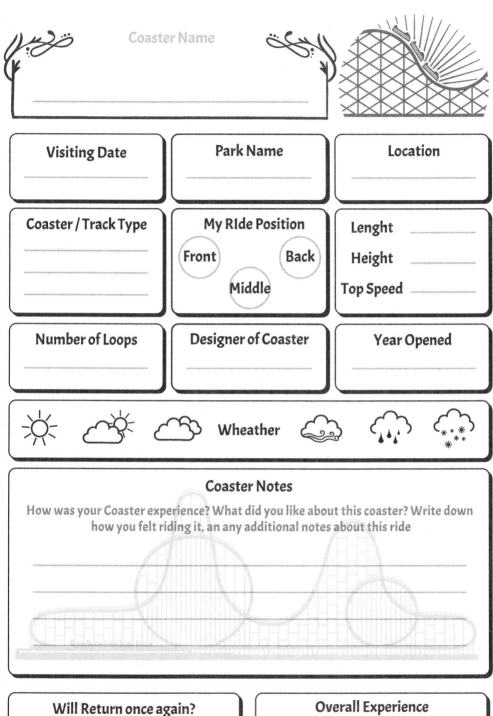

Coaster Name

Visiting Date	Park Name	Location

Coaster / Track Type

My RIde Position
Front Back Middle

Lenght
Height
Top Speed

Number of Loops	Designer of Coaster	Year Opened

Wheather

Coaster Notes

How was your Coaster experience? What did you like about this coaster? Write down how you felt riding it, an any additional notes about this ride

Will Return once again?

Yep / Nope

Overall Experience

☆ ☆ ☆ ☆ ☆

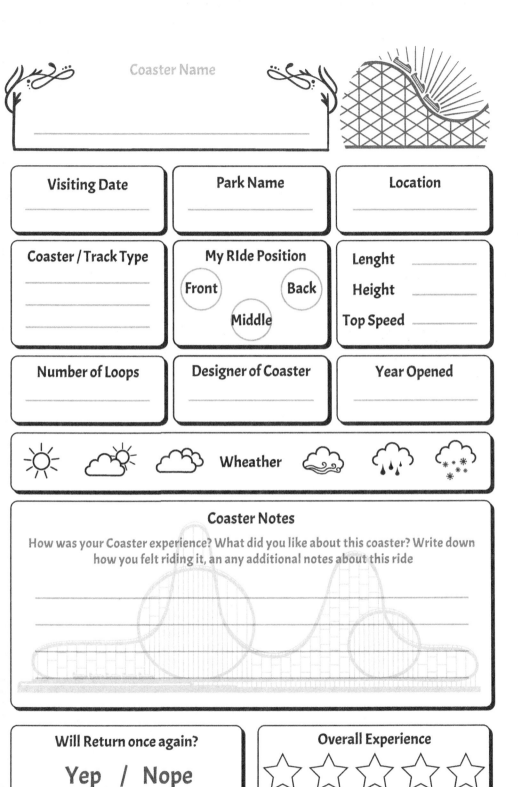

Coaster Name

Visiting Date

Park Name

Location

Coaster / Track Type

My RIde Position
Front   Back
Middle

Lenght
Height
Top Speed

Number of Loops

Designer of Coaster

Year Opened

Wheather

Coaster Notes

How was your Coaster experience? What did you like about this coaster? Write down how you felt riding it, an any additional notes about this ride

Will Return once again?

Yep / Nope

Overall Experience

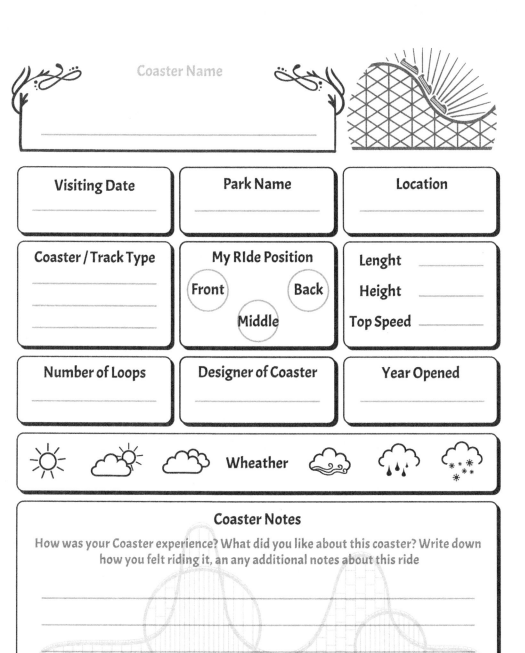

Coaster Name

Visiting Date

Park Name

Location

Coaster / Track Type

My RIde Position

Front   Back

Middle

Lenght

Height

Top Speed

Number of Loops

Designer of Coaster

Year Opened

Wheather

Coaster Notes

How was your Coaster experience? What did you like about this coaster? Write down how you felt riding it, an any additional notes about this ride

Will Return once again?

Yep / Nope

Overall Experience

Coaster Name

Visiting Date	Park Name	Location

Coaster / Track Type

My RIde Position
Front   Back
Middle

Lenght
Height
Top Speed

Number of Loops	Designer of Coaster	Year Opened

Wheather

Coaster Notes

How was your Coaster experience? What did you like about this coaster? Write down how you felt riding it, an any additional notes about this ride

Will Return once again?

Yep / Nope

Overall Experience

☆ ☆ ☆ ☆ ☆

Coaster Name

Visiting Date

Park Name

Location

Coaster / Track Type

My RIde Position

Front — Back

Middle

Lenght _____
Height _____
Top Speed _____

Number of Loops

Designer of Coaster

Year Opened

Wheather

Coaster Notes

How was your Coaster experience? What did you like about this coaster? Write down how you felt riding it, an any additional notes about this ride

Will Return once again?

Yep / Nope

Overall Experience

☆ ☆ ☆ ☆ ☆

Coaster Name

Visiting Date

Park Name

Location

Coaster / Track Type

My RIde Position

Front   Back

Middle

Lenght

Height

Top Speed

Number of Loops

Designer of Coaster

Year Opened

Wheather

Coaster Notes

How was your Coaster experience? What did you like about this coaster? Write down how you felt riding it, an any additional notes about this ride

Will Return once again?

Yep / Nope

Overall Experience

☆ ☆ ☆ ☆ ☆

Coaster Name

Visiting Date | Park Name | Location

Coaster / Track Type | My RIde Position | Lenght
 | Front   Back | Height
 | Middle | Top Speed

Number of Loops | Designer of Coaster | Year Opened

Wheather

Coaster Notes

How was your Coaster experience? What did you like about this coaster? Write down how you felt riding it, an any additional notes about this ride

Will Return once again?

Yep / Nope

Overall Experience

Coaster Name

Visiting Date

Park Name

Location

Coaster / Track Type

My RIde Position
(Front)   (Back)
(Middle)

Lenght
Height
Top Speed

Number of Loops

Designer of Coaster

Year Opened

Wheather

Coaster Notes

How was your Coaster experience? What did you like about this coaster? Write down how you felt riding it, an any additional notes about this ride

Will Return once again?

Yep / Nope

Overall Experience

Coaster Name

Visiting Date

Park Name

Location

Coaster / Track Type

My RIde Position
(Front)   (Back)
(Middle)

Lenght
Height
Top Speed

Number of Loops

Designer of Coaster

Year Opened

☀ ⛅ ☁ **Wheather** 🌬 🌧 🌨

Coaster Notes

How was your Coaster experience? What did you like about this coaster? Write down how you felt riding it, an any additional notes about this ride

Will Return once again?

Yep / Nope

Overall Experience
☆ ☆ ☆ ☆ ☆

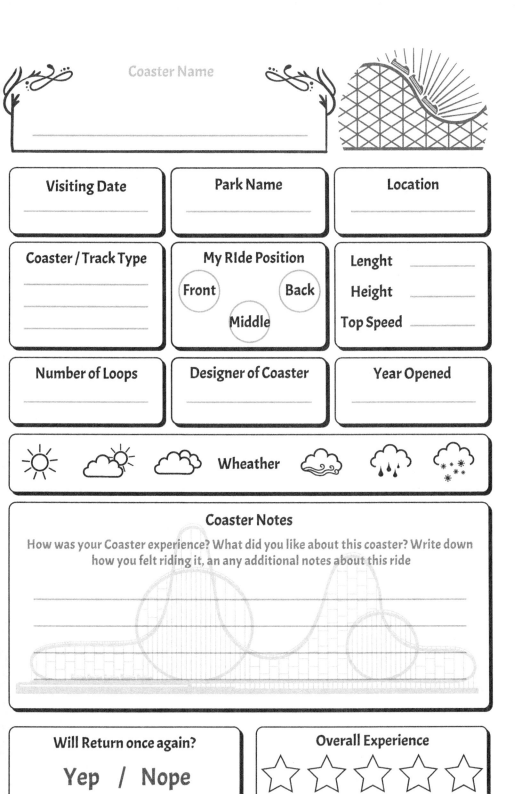

Coaster Name

_____

Visiting Date	**Park Name**	**Location**

Coaster / Track Type

My RIde Position
Front   Back
Middle

Lenght _____
Height _____
Top Speed _____

Number of Loops	**Designer of Coaster**	**Year Opened**

Wheather

Coaster Notes

How was your Coaster experience? What did you like about this coaster? Write down
how you felt riding it, an any additional notes about this ride

_____

_____

_____

Will Return once again?

Yep / Nope

Overall Experience

☆ ☆ ☆ ☆ ☆

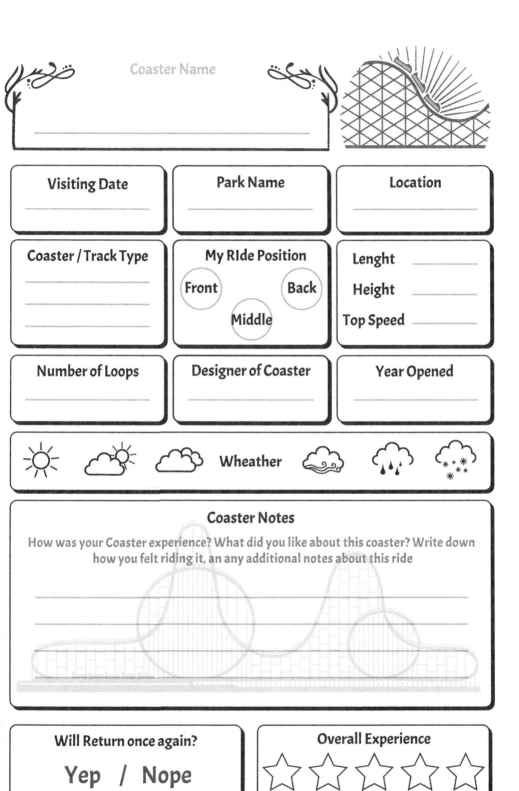

Coaster Name

Visiting Date	Park Name	Location

Coaster / Track Type

My RIde Position

Front   Back

Middle

Lenght
Height
Top Speed

Number of Loops	Designer of Coaster	Year Opened

Wheather

Coaster Notes

How was your Coaster experience? What did you like about this coaster? Write down how you felt riding it, an any additional notes about this ride

Will Return once again?

Yep / Nope

Overall Experience

☆ ☆ ☆ ☆ ☆

Coaster Name

Visiting Date	Park Name	Location

Coaster / Track Type

My Ride Position
- Front
- Back
- Middle

- Lenght
- Height
- Top Speed

Number of Loops | **Designer of Coaster** | **Year Opened**

Wheather

Coaster Notes
How was your Coaster experience? What did you like about this coaster? Write down how you felt riding it, an any additional notes about this ride

Will Return once again?

Yep / Nope

Overall Experience

☆ ☆ ☆ ☆ ☆

Coaster Name

| Visiting Date | Park Name | Location |

Coaster / Track Type

My RIde Position
Front   Back
Middle

Lenght
Height
Top Speed

| Number of Loops | Designer of Coaster | Year Opened |

Wheather

Coaster Notes

How was your Coaster experience? What did you like about this coaster? Write down how you felt riding it, an any additional notes about this ride

Will Return once again?

Yep / Nope

Overall Experience
☆ ☆ ☆ ☆ ☆

Coaster Name
_____

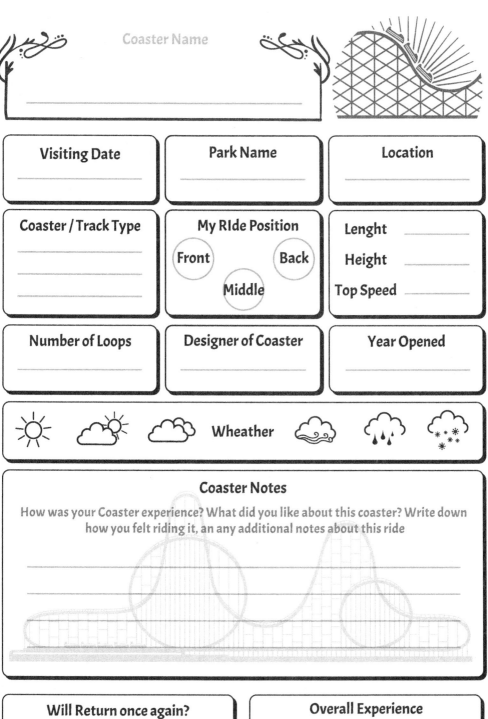

Visiting Date
_____

Park Name
_____

Location
_____

Coaster / Track Type
_____
_____

My RIde Position
(Front)   (Back)
(Middle)

Lenght _____
Height _____
Top Speed _____

Number of Loops
_____

Designer of Coaster
_____

Year Opened
_____

☀ ⛅ ☁ **Wheather** 🌫 🌧 🌨

Coaster Notes

How was your Coaster experience? What did you like about this coaster? Write down how you felt riding it, an any additional notes about this ride

_____
_____
_____

Will Return once again?

Yep / Nope

Overall Experience

Coaster Name

Visiting Date	Park Name	Location

Coaster / Track Type

My RIde Position
Front / Back / Middle

Lenght _____
Height _____
Top Speed _____

Number of Loops	Designer of Coaster	Year Opened

Wheather

Coaster Notes

How was your Coaster experience? What did you like about this coaster? Write down how you felt riding it, an any additional notes about this ride

Will Return once again?

Yep / Nope

Overall Experience

☆ ☆ ☆ ☆ ☆

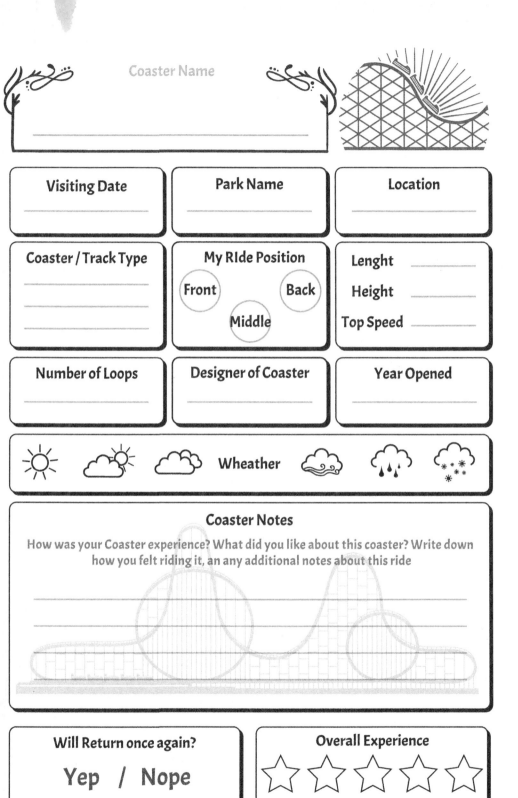

Coaster Name

Visiting Date	Park Name	Location

Coaster / Track Type	My RIde Position	Lenght
	Front Back	Height
	Middle	Top Speed

Number of Loops	Designer of Coaster	Year Opened

Wheather

Coaster Notes

How was your Coaster experience? What did you like about this coaster? Write down how you felt riding it, an any additional notes about this ride

Will Return once again?	Overall Experience
Yep / Nope	☆ ☆ ☆ ☆ ☆

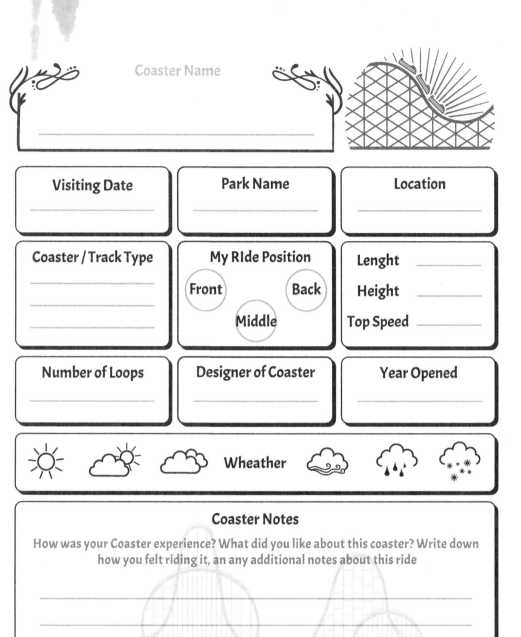

Coaster Name

| Visiting Date | Park Name | Location |

Coaster / Track Type	My RIde Position	Lenght
	Front — Back — Middle	Height
		Top Speed

| Number of Loops | Designer of Coaster | Year Opened |

Wheather

Coaster Notes

How was your Coaster experience? What did you like about this coaster? Write down how you felt riding it, an any additional notes about this ride

Will Return once again?

Yep / Nope

Overall Experience

☆ ☆ ☆ ☆ ☆

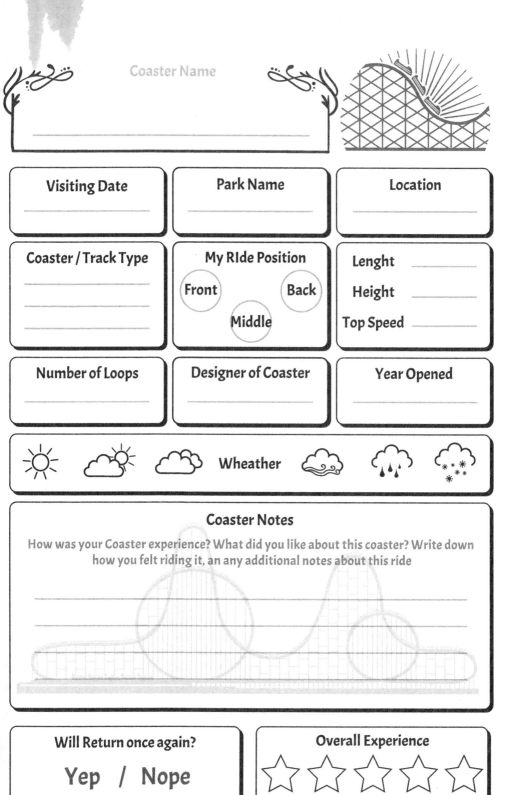

Coaster Name

| **Visiting Date** | **Park Name** | **Location** |

Coaster / Track Type

My RIde Position

Front   Back

Middle

Lenght
Height
Top Speed

| **Number of Loops** | **Designer of Coaster** | **Year Opened** |

Wheather

Coaster Notes

How was your Coaster experience? What did you like about this coaster? Write down how you felt riding it, an any additional notes about this ride

Will Return once again?

Yep / Nope

Overall Experience

☆ ☆ ☆ ☆ ☆

Coaster Name

| Visiting Date | Park Name | Location |

| Coaster / Track Type | My Ride Position — Front / Back / Middle | Lenght / Height / Top Speed |

| Number of Loops | Designer of Coaster | Year Opened |

Wheather

Coaster Notes

How was your Coaster experience? What did you like about this coaster? Write down how you felt riding it, an any additional notes about this ride

| Will Return once again? — Yep / Nope | Overall Experience |

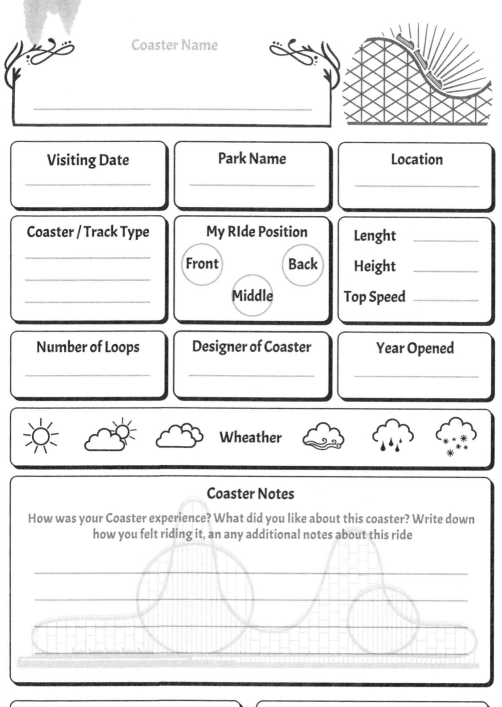

Coaster Name

_____

Visiting Date	Park Name	Location

Coaster / Track Type

My RIde Position
Front | Back
Middle

Lenght _____
Height _____
Top Speed _____

Number of Loops	Designer of Coaster	Year Opened

Wheather

Coaster Notes

How was your Coaster experience? What did you like about this coaster? Write down how you felt riding it, an any additional notes about this ride

Will Return once again?

Yep / Nope

Overall Experience

☆☆☆☆☆

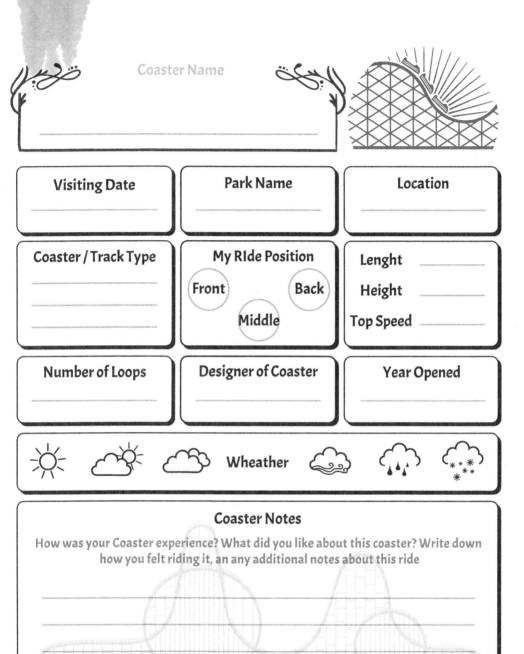

Coaster Name

Visiting Date	Park Name	Location

Coaster / Track Type	My RIde Position	Lenght
	Front Back	Height
	Middle	Top Speed

Number of Loops	Designer of Coaster	Year Opened

Wheather

Coaster Notes

How was your Coaster experience? What did you like about this coaster? Write down how you felt riding it, an any additional notes about this ride

Will Return once again?	Overall Experience
Yep / Nope	☆☆☆☆☆

Coaster Name

_____

Visiting Date	**Park Name**	**Location**

Coaster / Track Type	**My Ride Position** Front Back Middle	**Lenght** _____ **Height** _____ **Top Speed** _____

Number of Loops	**Designer of Coaster**	**Year Opened**

   **Wheather**

Coaster Notes

How was your Coaster experience? What did you like about this coaster? Write down how you felt riding it, an any additional notes about this ride

_____
_____
_____

Will Return once again? Yep / Nope	**Overall Experience** 

Coaster Name

Visiting Date	Park Name	Location

Coaster / Track Type

My RIde Position
Front   Back
Middle

Lenght
Height
Top Speed

Number of Loops	Designer of Coaster	Year Opened

Wheather

Coaster Notes

How was your Coaster experience? What did you like about this coaster? Write down how you felt riding it, an any additional notes about this ride

Will Return once again?

Yep / Nope

Overall Experience
☆☆☆☆☆

Coaster Name

_____

Visiting Date	Park Name	Location

Coaster / Track Type	My Ride Position Front Back Middle	Lenght ____ Height ____ Top Speed ____

Number of Loops	Designer of Coaster	Year Opened

Wheather

Coaster Notes

How was your Coaster experience? What did you like about this coaster? Write down how you felt riding it, an any additional notes about this ride

_____
_____
_____

Will Return once again? Yep / Nope	Overall Experience ☆ ☆ ☆ ☆ ☆

Coaster Name

_____

Visiting Date	**Park Name**	**Location**

Coaster / Track Type

My RIde Position
(Front)   (Back)
(Middle)

Lenght _____
Height _____
Top Speed _____

Number of Loops	**Designer of Coaster**	**Year Opened**

Wheather

Coaster Notes

How was your Coaster experience? What did you like about this coaster? Write down how you felt riding it, an any additional notes about this ride

_____
_____
_____

Will Return once again?

Yep / Nope

Overall Experience

☆ ☆ ☆ ☆ ☆

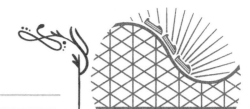

Coaster Name

Visiting Date	Park Name	Location

Coaster / Track Type	My Ride Position	Lenght
	Front Back	Height
	Middle	Top Speed

Number of Loops	Designer of Coaster	Year Opened

   Wheather

Coaster Notes

How was your Coaster experience? What did you like about this coaster? Write down how you felt riding it, an any additional notes about this ride

Will Return once again?	Overall Experience
Yep / Nope	

Coaster Name

Visiting Date	Park Name	Location

Coaster / Track Type

My RIde Position

Front   Back
Middle

Lenght
Height
Top Speed

Number of Loops	Designer of Coaster	Year Opened

Wheather

Coaster Notes

How was your Coaster experience? What did you like about this coaster? Write down how you felt riding it, an any additional notes about this ride

Will Return once again?

Yep / Nope

Overall Experience

☆ ☆ ☆ ☆ ☆

Coaster Name

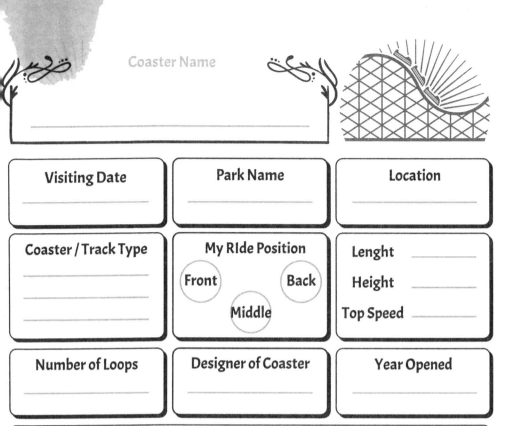

Visiting Date

Park Name

Location

Coaster / Track Type

My RIde Position
Front   Back
Middle

Lenght
Height
Top Speed

Number of Loops

Designer of Coaster

Year Opened

   Wheather

Coaster Notes

How was your Coaster experience? What did you like about this coaster? Write down how you felt riding it, an any additional notes about this ride

Will Return once again?

Yep / Nope

Overall Experience

Coaster Name

Visiting Date	Park Name	Location

Coaster / Track Type	My RIde Position	Lenght
	Front — Back — Middle	Height — Top Speed

Number of Loops	Designer of Coaster	Year Opened

Wheather

Coaster Notes

How was your Coaster experience? What did you like about this coaster? Write down how you felt riding it, an any additional notes about this ride

---

Will Return once again?

Yep / Nope

Overall Experience

☆ ☆ ☆ ☆ ☆

Coaster Name

_____

Visiting Date	Park Name	Location

Coaster / Track Type	My Ride Position	Lenght _____
	Front Back	Height _____
	Middle	Top Speed _____

Number of Loops	Designer of Coaster	Year Opened

   Wheather

Coaster Notes

How was your Coaster experience? What did you like about this coaster? Write down how you felt riding it, an any additional notes about this ride

_____
_____
_____

Will Return once again?	Overall Experience
Yep / Nope	☆ ☆ ☆ ☆ ☆

Coaster Name

___

Visiting Date
___

Park Name
___

Location
___

Coaster / Track Type
___

My RIde Position
(Front)   (Back)
(Middle)

Lenght ___
Height ___
Top Speed ___

Number of Loops
___

Designer of Coaster
___

Year Opened
___

Wheather

Coaster Notes

How was your Coaster experience? What did you like about this coaster? Write down how you felt riding it, an any additional notes about this ride

___
___
___
___

Will Return once again?

Yep / Nope

Overall Experience

☆ ☆ ☆ ☆ ☆

Coaster Name

Visiting Date

Park Name

Location

Coaster / Track Type

My Ride Position
- Front
- Back
- Middle

Lenght

Height

Top Speed

Number of Loops

Designer of Coaster

Year Opened

  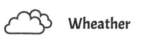 **Wheather**

Coaster Notes

How was your Coaster experience? What did you like about this coaster? Write down how you felt riding it, an any additional notes about this ride

---

Will Return once again?

Yep / Nope

Overall Experience

Coaster Name

_____

Visiting Date

Park Name

Location

Coaster / Track Type

My RIde Position
Front   Back
Middle

Lenght _____
Height _____
Top Speed _____

Number of Loops

Designer of Coaster

Year Opened

Wheather

Coaster Notes
How was your Coaster experience? What did you like about this coaster? Write down how you felt riding it, an any additional notes about this ride

Will Return once again?
Yep / Nope

Overall Experience
☆ ☆ ☆ ☆ ☆

Coaster Name

_____

Visiting Date	**Park Name**	**Location**

Coaster / Track Type	**My RIde Position** Front Back Middle	**Lenght** _____ **Height** _____ **Top Speed** _____

Number of Loops	**Designer of Coaster**	**Year Opened**

   **Wheather**

Coaster Notes

How was your Coaster experience? What did you like about this coaster? Write down how you felt riding it, an any additional notes about this ride

_____

_____

Will Return once again?

Yep / Nope

Overall Experience

Coaster Name

_____

Visiting Date

_____

Park Name

_____

Location

_____

Coaster / Track Type

_____
_____
_____

My RIde Position

(Front)   (Back)

(Middle)

Lenght _____

Height _____

Top Speed _____

Number of Loops

_____

Designer of Coaster

_____

Year Opened

_____

Wheather

Coaster Notes

How was your Coaster experience? What did you like about this coaster? Write down how you felt riding it, an any additional notes about this ride

_____
_____
_____

Will Return once again?

Yep / Nope

Overall Experience

☆ ☆ ☆ ☆ ☆

Coaster Name
_____

Visiting Date

Park Name

Location

Coaster / Track Type

My RIde Position
(Front)   (Back)
(Middle)

Lenght _____
Height _____
Top Speed _____

Number of Loops

Designer of Coaster

Year Opened

☀️ ⛅ ☁️   **Wheather**   🌬️ 🌧️ 🌨️

Coaster Notes
How was your Coaster experience? What did you like about this coaster? Write down how you felt riding it, an any additional notes about this ride

_____
_____
_____
_____

Will Return once again?
Yep / Nope

Overall Experience
☆ ☆ ☆ ☆ ☆

Coaster Name

Visiting Date	Park Name	Location

Coaster / Track Type	My RIde Position	Lenght
	Front Back	Height
	Middle	Top Speed

Number of Loops	Designer of Coaster	Year Opened

Wheather

Coaster Notes

How was your Coaster experience? What did you like about this coaster? Write down how you felt riding it, an any additional notes about this ride

Will Return once again?	Overall Experience
Yep / Nope	☆ ☆ ☆ ☆ ☆

Coaster Name

Visiting Date	Park Name	Location

Coaster / Track Type

My RIde Position
- Front
- Back
- Middle

Lenght
Height
Top Speed

Number of Loops	Designer of Coaster	Year Opened

   Wheather

Coaster Notes

How was your Coaster experience? What did you like about this coaster? Write down how you felt riding it, an any additional notes about this ride

Will Return once again?

Yep / Nope

Overall Experience

Coaster Name

Visiting Date

Park Name

Location

Coaster / Track Type

My RIde Position

Front   Back

Middle

Lenght

Height

Top Speed

Number of Loops

Designer of Coaster

Year Opened

Wheather

Coaster Notes

How was your Coaster experience? What did you like about this coaster? Write down how you felt riding it, an any additional notes about this ride

Will Return once again?

Yep / Nope

Overall Experience

☆ ☆ ☆ ☆ ☆

Coaster Name

_____

Visiting Date
_____

Park Name
_____

Location
_____

Coaster / Track Type
_____
_____
_____

My Ride Position
(Front)   (Back)
(Middle)

Lenght _____
Height _____
Top Speed _____

Number of Loops
_____

Designer of Coaster
_____

Year Opened
_____

   **Wheather**

Coaster Notes

How was your Coaster experience? What did you like about this coaster? Write down how you felt riding it, an any additional notes about this ride

_____
_____
_____
_____

Will Return once again?

Yep / Nope

Overall Experience

Coaster Name

Visiting Date	Park Name	Location

Coaster / Track Type

My RIde Position
Front   Back
Middle

Lenght
Height
Top Speed

Number of Loops	Designer of Coaster	Year Opened

Wheather

Coaster Notes

How was your Coaster experience? What did you like about this coaster? Write down how you felt riding it, an any additional notes about this ride

Will Return once again?

Yep / Nope

Overall Experience
☆☆☆☆☆

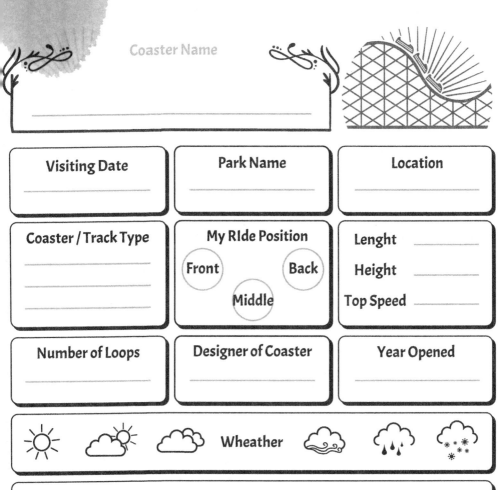

Coaster Name

Visiting Date

Park Name

Location

Coaster / Track Type

My RIde Position
Front   Back
Middle

Lenght
Height
Top Speed

Number of Loops

Designer of Coaster

Year Opened

Wheather

Coaster Notes

How was your Coaster experience? What did you like about this coaster? Write down how you felt riding it, an any additional notes about this ride

Will Return once again?

Yep / Nope

Overall Experience

Coaster Name

_____

Visiting Date
_____

Park Name
_____

Location
_____

Coaster / Track Type
_____
_____

My RIde Position
(Front)   (Back)
(Middle)

Lenght _____
Height _____
Top Speed _____

Number of Loops
_____

Designer of Coaster
_____

Year Opened
_____

Wheather

Coaster Notes

How was your Coaster experience? What did you like about this coaster? Write down how you felt riding it, an any additional notes about this ride

_____
_____
_____
_____

Will Return once again?

Yep / Nope

Overall Experience

☆ ☆ ☆ ☆ ☆

Printed in Great Britain
by Amazon